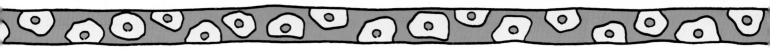

THE MAYA

Peter Chrisp

Wayland

Look into the Past

Series editor: Joanna Bentley
Series designer: David West
Book designer: Stephen Wheele

First published in 1994 by Wayland (Publishers) Limited,
61 Western Road, Hove, East Sussex, BN3 1JD, England

British Library Cataloguing in Publication Data
Chrisp, Peter
Maya. – (Look into the Past series)
I. Title II. Series
972.800497

ISBN 0 7502 1066 4

Typeset by Dorchester Typesetting Group Ltd., Dorset,
England.
Printed and bound in Italy by L.E.G.O. S.p.A., Vicenza,
Italy.

Picture acknowledgements
The publishers wish to thank the following for providing the
photographs in this book: E T Archive 14 (left, British
Museum), 22 (Museum of Mankind, London), 23 (Museum
of Mankind), 26; Werner Forman Archive cover, 5, 6
(National Museum of Anthropology, Mexico City), 8, 10, 11
(bottom, Dallas Museum of Art, USA) 12, 13, 14 (right), 16
(courtesy Sotheby's, New York), 17 (top, National Museum
of Anthropology, Mexico City), 19, 20 (both; left, Edward H
Merrin Gallery, New York), 21 (National Museum of
Anthropology, Mexico City), 24 (National Museum of
Anthropology, Mexico City), 25 (all; top left, National
Museum of Anthropology, Mexico City), 27 (bottom, Dr
Kurt Stavenhagen Collection, Mexico City); Michael
Holford cover, 7, 11 (top), 17 (bottom, British Museum), 18
(British Museum); South American Pictures 4 (Tony
Morrison), 9 (top, Tony Morrison, bottom, Robert Francis),
29 (top, Kimball Morrison, bottom, Robert Francis).
Artwork by Stephen Wheele.

CONTENTS

Words that appear in *bold italic* in the text are explained in the glossary on page 30.

THE MAYA

Deep in the forests of Mexico and Central America, there are the ruins of ancient cities. These cities were built more than a thousand years ago, by a people called the Maya. The Maya were wonderful artists and craftspeople. Although they had no metal tools or wheeled transport, they built tall *pyramids* and palaces. They were skilled in *astronomy* and mathematics. They invented a complicated and beautiful system of writing, which they used to make books and stone carvings.

Maya civilization was at its greatest between the years AD 300 and 900. At the end of this period, many of the cities were abandoned. The forests took over. Even so, the Maya themselves did not disappear. There are still up to four million of them living in Mexico, Guatemala, Belize and Honduras.

◀ Here is just one of the Maya cities, Tikal, with its tall *temples* rising above the forest. At the height of its power in the 800s, Tikal was an enormous place. It was home to about 50,000 people.

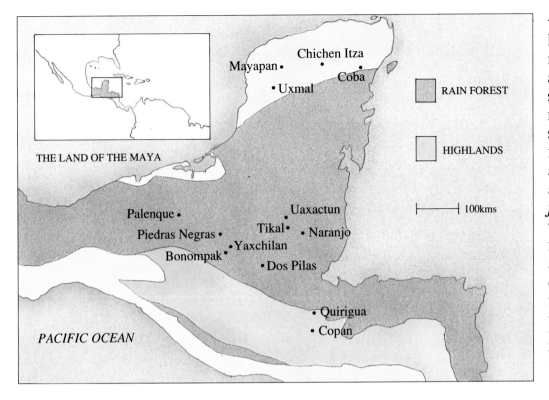

THE LAND OF THE MAYA

PACIFIC OCEAN

Chichen Itza
Mayapan •
• Coba
• Uxmal

RAIN FOREST

HIGHLANDS

├──────┤ 100kms

Palenque •
Uaxactun •
Piedras Negras •
Tikal • • Naranjo
• Yaxchilan
Bonompak •
• Dos Pilas

• Quirigua
• Copan

◀ This map shows the land of the Maya. The northern part is dry and scrubby. In the south, there are high mountains, surrounded by pine forests. The largest area, however, is hot and steamy *rain forest*. This is a place where it rains heavily from May to October and is dry for the rest of the year. It was in this rain forest area that most of the great Maya cities were built.

The rain forest was ▶ the home for many different animals, like the monkey on this Maya vase. There were colourful birds – parrots and macaws – which the Maya hunted with blow guns for their bright feathers. There were deer and tapirs, which were caught for meat. To the Maya, the most important animal was the jaguar, the big, fierce, spotted cat that hunted by night. You will come across jaguars several times as you look through this book.

We know what the ancient Maya looked like, thanks to their paintings and sculptures. This head of a noble from Palenque shows one of the strangest things about the Maya – their flat foreheads. Babies had their skulls tightly bound to make the soft bone develop a flat shape. To the Maya, a flat skull was a sign of beauty.

As well as having flat skulls, Maya nobles built up the tops of their noses with clay, making a long ridge. They also filed their teeth into different shapes. These ideas of beauty seem very odd to us nowadays, but the Maya would have found us just as strange-looking as we find them!

CITIES

The Maya never belonged to a single nation. Instead, they lived in many separate kingdoms, which often went to war with each other. Each kingdom was based on a city which ruled the surrounding countryside. The centre of a Maya city was a large area for religious *ceremonies*, dances and processions. This ceremonial area included temples, royal palaces and big open squares. Outside the ceremonial area were the houses and workshops of the ordinary people. These buildings were probably built of wood rather than stone and so have not survived.

◀ This is the palace building at Palenque. It was built over a long period by different kings, each adding something new.

The biggest buildings in Maya cities were the pyramids. These were mostly built as burial places for dead kings.

This pyramid, at Uxmal, is enormous. It has a long flight of stairs up one side, leading to a small temple building at the top. Imagine the work it took to build this pyramid! The fact that kings could make their people build such huge things for them shows how powerful they were.▼

◀ This is the tomb chamber of King Pacal ('Shield') of Palenque, deep inside his pyramid. Pacal died on 31 August 683, after ruling Palenque for sixty-eight years. The body of the dead king lay under the great stone slab. This slab, or lid, is carved with a picture of Pacal travelling into the **Underworld** at the moment of his death.

▼ This little building is a temple, a place for worship. Inside temples like this, Maya kings and nobles performed ceremonies in honour of the gods. In pyramid temples they prayed to the dead king, who was buried in the heart of the pyramid, beneath their feet. There are two small dark rooms in this temple. The back wall of the inner room is carved with the face of the sun god, and so today this building is known as the Temple of the Sun.

This is a temple and an observatory, a place for looking at the stars in the night sky. From the top of this building in the city of Chichen Itza, the Maya studied the movements of the planets and the stars. They were brilliant astronomers – they could predict *eclipses* as well as the movements of the planet Venus. This planet can be seen in the morning sky for 263 days. Then it disappears from view for around sixty days, reappearing in the evening sky for another 263 days before vanishing again.

Their reasons for studying the sky were religious. To the Maya, the planet Venus was a god. It was also a very dangerous god, a bringer of war and death – when it appeared for the first time in the sky at dawn, Maya warriors set out to fight battles.

▼ This vase painting shows the heavy padding that the ball players wore, to protect them from the big, solid rubber ball. As you can see, they also wore elaborate head-dresses. Players were not allowed to touch the ball with their hands or feet; instead, they hit it with their hips, shoulders and chest. If you try doing this yourself with a football, you will see how difficult it is!

▲ Here is something that the Maya built in almost all of their cities. Do you have any idea what it is?

It is a ballcourt, a place where a game was played with a rubber ball. Players had to keep the ball bouncing against the sloping side of the court without it landing in the long central alley. The ball game was much more than a sport. It was also a religious ceremony played in honour of the gods.

GODS

The Maya believed in dozens of gods, each controlling a different part of life. It was thanks to these gods that life on earth was possible. The sun god gave light and warmth. The rain god brought the yearly downpour in May which fed the crops. The maize god made the seeds burst into life.

As well as giving life, the gods could destroy it. The rain god could cause floods and storms. The sun god could dry up the fields. The Maya had many religious ceremonies which they held to please the gods and win their help. Sometimes, they dressed up as the gods and danced to music. They also offered food to them – maize cakes, meat and, the most precious food of all, human blood.

◀ This fierce-looking face belongs to the sun god, Ahaw Kin ('Lord Sun'). When the sun disappeared at nightfall, the Maya believed that the god was travelling down into the Underworld. Then the sun god became the Jaguar God of the Underworld. He was an especially important god to Maya kings. When they died, they were buried wearing masks showing the god's face.

Look at the carving on this wall, in the ▶ Maya city of Uxmal. Can you see faces, with big teeth and round eyes? These faces belong to the rain god, who was worshipped by many Mexican peoples – he was later an important god to the *Aztecs*. His name was Tlaloc.

▼ This is a war god. It may be the sun god, who became the Jaguar God of the Underworld at night. Can you see the warriors who stand on either side of the central figure? This object is an *incense* burner. The Maya burned sweet-smelling incense in the round basin at the top. The smoke carried their offering to the gods.

▲ This is the god of maize, the main food of the Maya. Sometimes he was called Yum Caax, which means 'Lord of the Forest Bush'. He was always shown as a handsome young man with long hair. Sometimes he had maize leaves growing out of the top of his head. He was the friendliest of all the Maya gods.

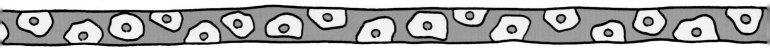

At the bottom of this vase you can see the face of another god. His name is not known, but he was very important in the Maya city, Palenque. He was always shown with fishy features – a shark's tooth, a fin on his cheek and a barbel (a dangling piece of flesh) at the corner of his mouth. The Palenque rulers thought of this god as one of the founders of their city. They believed that he had been born in the year 2360 BC – three thousand years before their own time – and that he still watched over Palenque.

WRITING

The Maya were the only *native American* people to invent a complete writing system. Other peoples, such as the Aztecs, used picture writing to record names, dates and important events. But only the Maya were able to write complete sentences.

Maya writing appears in several forms. It was painted in books, on pottery and on walls and it was carved on jewellery and on stone. Buildings and monuments had the name of the ruling king and the date carved on them. A lot of Maya writing is to do with time, which the Maya kept track of using a number of complicated calendars.

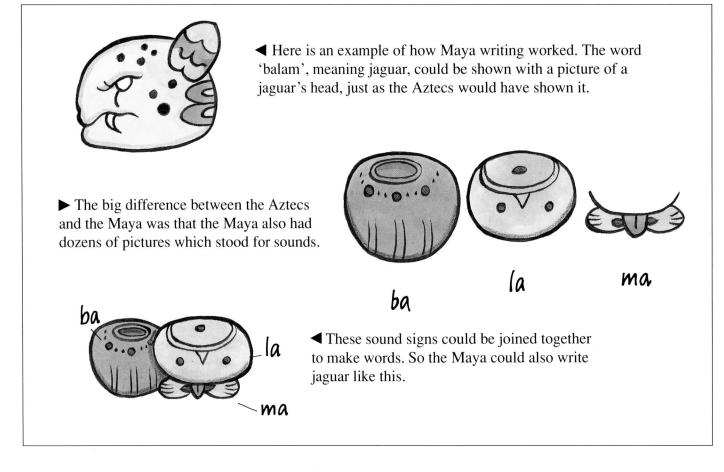

◀ Here is an example of how Maya writing worked. The word 'balam', meaning jaguar, could be shown with a picture of a jaguar's head, just as the Aztecs would have shown it.

▶ The big difference between the Aztecs and the Maya was that the Maya also had dozens of pictures which stood for sounds.

ba

la

ma

◀ These sound signs could be joined together to make words. So the Maya could also write jaguar like this.

ba

la

ma

Thanks to sound signs, like the ones here, the Maya could write down any word they wanted and they could join the words together to make sentences.

▼ Here are some pages from a Maya book. Only four books have been found, but once there were many hundreds of them. The surviving books are all religious guides, explaining the movements of the planet Venus and the roles played by different gods at different times of the year. Maya nobles believed they could use these books to foretell the future. The black figure on these pages is the god of trade and cacao beans, which were used as money by the Maya.

▲ Only noble men and women knew how to read and write. Can you see the book this noble woman is reading on her lap? Maya books were painted on paper made from fig tree bark, folded up like a concertina.

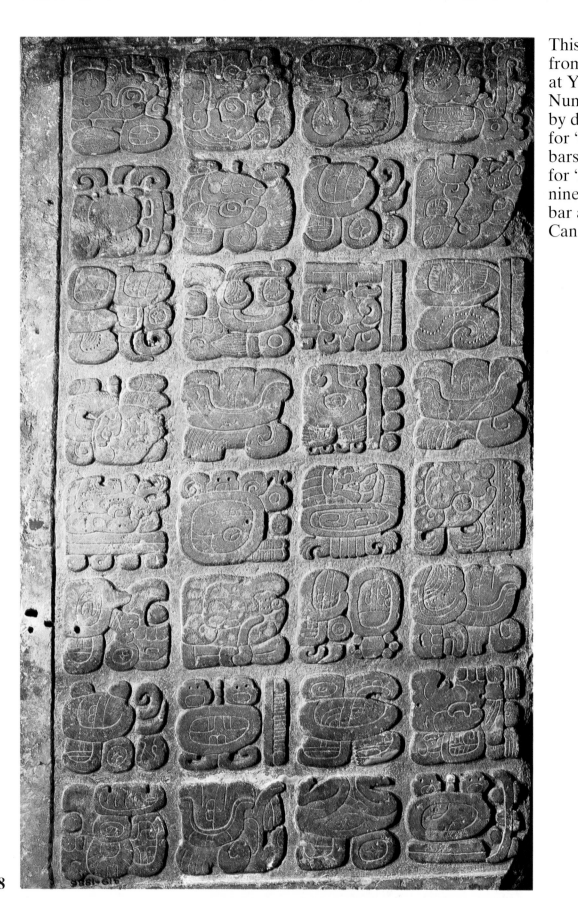

This is a Maya date, from a carving found at Yaxchilan. Numbers are shown by dots, each standing for 'one', and upright bars, each standing for 'five'. The number nine is shown by one bar and four dots. Can you find it?

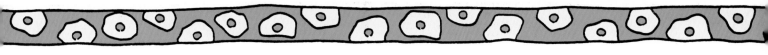

KINGS

Each Maya city was ruled by a king, known as the ahaw (lord) or the makina (great sun lord). The king was both a war leader and a sort of priest. He looked after his people by performing religious ceremonies – usually involving drawing his own blood. The Maya believed that royal blood had special powers. Blood-letting ceremonies allowed their kings to get in touch with the gods and win their help.

We know a lot about Maya kings, thanks to the standing stones they set up in their cities. These objects, called 'stone trees', were carved to mark important dates in the calendar and royal blood-letting ceremonies. They also carried a portrait of the king who had set them up.

◀ This carved piece of jade once hung from the belt of a Maya king. It shows the king himself in the act of being made ruler – like a coronation ceremony. He stands on a bench held up by two prisoners, who will be *sacrificed* as part of the ceremony. In his arms he holds a royal sceptre, a long bar which is a sign of his rank as a king.

▼ This is a king's drinking cup, used to hold chocolate – drunk by only the most important Maya. Paintings on royal drinking cups like this are full of details of the life of kings. Look at this king, receiving food from the figure on the left. Like rulers all over the world, Maya kings showed their power by sitting on raised seats – thrones. This king's throne is draped with skins of jaguars. To the Maya, the jaguar was like a king of the forest – jaguar skins were a mark of power and royalty.

Maya kings were very powerful people when they were alive. Their power was believed to carry on even after death – then they were thought to be like gods. This beautiful mask was worn by the dead king Pacal, as he lay in his tomb at Palenque. The mask is made from jade, the most precious material that the Maya knew. The T-shaped teeth are a sign of the sun god.

Maya kings and nobles marked important occasions by drawing their blood and offering it to the gods. The carvings on these pages show how, and why, this was done.

This carving shows ▶ Lady Xoc, wife of King Shield Jaguar of Yaxchilan, in the act of drawing her blood. Her husband stands over her with a flaming torch – the ceremony must have taken place at night, or in the dark room of a temple. She kneels and pulls a rope, studded with thorns, through her tongue. The blood is collected on rolled up bark paper, in a basket on the floor. Once she has made her offering, the king will draw his own blood. The writing tells us that this took place on 28 October 709.

◀ The second carving shows the next stage of the ceremony. Lady Xoc has set fire to the blood-soaked paper, which is in the bowl at the bottom. As the smoke rises, it turns into a giant snake. The snake's jaws open and out comes a royal *ancestor* – a dead Maya king who has become a god. By shedding their blood, Lady Xoc and Shield Jaguar have summoned up a figure from the world of the gods.

WAR

As well as offering his own blood to the gods, it was a king's duty to offer the blood of prisoners, captured in battle. All important events included human sacrifice. As a result, Maya cities were often at war with each other to capture prisoners for sacrifice. The king was expected to lead his warriors in person and to capture prisoners with his own hands.

◀ Maya kings were so proud of their success in warfare that they had carvings set up showing them in action. This is Shield Jaguar again, getting ready for battle in the year 724. As his name suggests, this king went into battle dressed as a fierce jaguar. His wife hands him his shield and his jaguar head-dress.

Maya warriors ▶ dressed to look as frightening as possible. They went into battle shouting, blowing long wooden trumpets and pulling terrifying faces. Their aim in battle was not to kill their enemies but to capture them. Everyone respected a warrior who had captured a large number of prisoners.

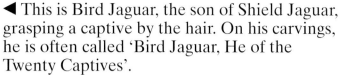
◀ This is Bird Jaguar, the son of Shield Jaguar, grasping a captive by the hair. On his carvings, he is often called 'Bird Jaguar, He of the Twenty Captives'.

The risk for kings like Bird Jaguar was that they themselves could be captured and sacrificed. This would be a disaster for the city which lost its king, but a great triumph for the capturing side.

▲ This vase painting shows the captives, held by the hair, led in triumph after the battle. They are being taken to the city of the winning warriors, where they will be sacrificed. Prisoners were killed in many different ways. Sometimes they were forced to play the ball game before their deaths. Then their heads might be chopped off with an axe or they might be thrown from the top of a temple.

25

DAILY LIFE

While Maya rulers were busy with religious ceremonies and raids for captives, the lives of ordinary people were very different. They were mainly farmers, growing maize, *squashes* and beans. Most of the farm work was done by the men, while the women made clothes, prepared food and looked after the children.

Mothers carried their young children on their backs, as you can see in this modern copy of a scene from a Maya book. This left their hands free for weaving cloth or making meals.

If you visited an ancient Maya village, you would see lots of people carrying things on their backs, often strapped to their long flat foreheads. All goods were carried by people on foot – there were no animals, such as horses, big enough to carry loads or pull a cart.

◀ Here is a farmer, copied from a Maya book. He is planting maize in holes made with a digging stick. The Maya had two ways of growing maize. In swampy areas and on the shores of rivers and lakes, they cut canals, heaping the earth up into raised fields. Each year, they piled fresh earth from the canal bed on to the field. This kept the field *fertile*, year after year.

The second method was used in the forests. In the dry season, the men cleared an area of forest using stone axes. Then they burned the cut bush and planted maize in the ashes. When the rains arrived the maize sprouted. This is known as 'slash and burn' farming. Fields made like this are only fertile for a couple of years. Then a new area of forest must be cut down and burned.

Maya women were ▶ skilled at spinning and weaving cloth from cotton to make clothes and blankets. This woman is weaving cloth. One end of her loom is strapped around her back, like a belt. When she wants to tighten the threads, she simply leans back. Maya women today still weave cotton like this.

27

WHAT HAPPENED TO THE MAYA?

In the years 850 to 900 something happened to the Maya. All over the central rain forest, cities were abandoned. We know when people left them because of the dates on buildings and monuments. After the year 889, no more dates were carved. No one knows for certain what happened. Perhaps there was a famine, caused by bad weather or by farmers using up too much land. Perhaps the constant wars were to blame.

This did not mean the end of the Maya. In the south and in the far north, people continued to live in rival cities. They no longer carved dates in stone, but they went on making painted books.

In the 1520s Spaniards arrived and conquered the land of the Maya. They banned sacrifice and burned almost all the Maya books they could find. Soon the Maya had lost the ability to read and write using their own letters. For more than a hundred years scholars have been trying to understand how Maya writing worked. Yet it is only in the last twenty years that big breakthroughs have been made. Finally, we can now read again the words written by the ancient Maya. This rolled out scene from a vase, found in a royal tomb in 1904, shows a king receiving gifts of food and cloth from less powerful lords. The writing above the figures tells us their names.

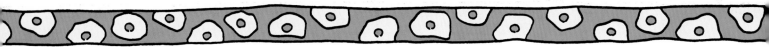

◀ This is the house of a Maya family, living in Mexico today. Thanks to wall-paintings, we know that the ancient Maya lived in houses just like this. You can see that it has a base of stone with wooden walls. There is a high roof thatched with grasses. This slopes steeply, as protection against the heavy downpour of the rainy season.

Despite everything, ▶ Maya civilization was not completely destroyed. The Maya of today still use traditional farming methods. These farmers in Guatemala are growing crops in raised fields, just as the Maya have done for more than a thousand years.

29

GLOSSARY

Ancestor   A person far back in a family's history. The word means someone who has 'gone before'.

Astronomy   The study of the stars and planets in space.

Aztecs   A people who conquered much of Mexico, to the west of the Maya, between 1400 and 1521.

Blood-letting   Removing blood from the body.

Ceremony   Any solemn or religious act which has to be performed in a set way, such as a marriage service.

Eclipses   Eclipses of the sun happen when the moon passes between the sun and the Earth, blocking out some of the sun's light. Eclipses of the moon happen when the Earth passes between the moon and the sun, and casts its shadow on the moon's surface. The Maya were terrified of eclipses and they learned to predict them.

Famine   A great shortage of food.

Fertile   Soil that produces good crops.

Incense   Any gum or spice which gives off a sweet smell when it is burned. Maya incense was copal, a sticky substance from certain trees.

Loom   A machine for weaving thread into cloth.

Native Americans   People who lived in the Americas before the coming of Europeans.

Pyramid   A tall building with sloping sides, a narrow top and a broad base. Maya pyramids were often built as tombs for dead kings.

Rain forest   A type of forest found in hot places with heavy rainfall. They are in the tropics, the hot area around the Equator (an imaginary line drawn around the centre of the Earth).

Sacrifice   Killing a person or an animal as an offering to a god or goddess.

Squashes   Vegetables, like marrows, which have hard rinds and soft flesh inside.

Temples   Buildings where gods and goddesses are worshipped.

Underworld   The Maya believed that there was another world, beneath our own, where the dead live and where the sun travelled to at night. It was a dark and frightening place – one of its names was Xibalba, 'place of fright'. It had entrances in caves and at the bottom of lakes.

IMPORTANT DATES

All dates are AD

c 300 Maya civilization flourishes throughout Central America and Eastern Mexico

615-683 The reign of Pacal, king of Palenque

681-742 The reign of Shield Jaguar, king of Yaxchilan

800 The wall-paintings of Bonompak are made

850-900 Many Maya cities are abandoned

889 Last date carved on a Maya monument

1523 Spaniards begin conquest of the Maya cities

1697 Spaniards conquer Tayasal, the last Maya stronghold

PRONUNCIATION

Place names in the Maya homelands are in either Spanish or Mayan. As a general rule, 'x' sounds like 'sh' and 'a' sounds like 'ah'. Here are some names you may find difficult:

Chichen Itza: chee-chain-ee-tsah

Palenque: pah-lain-kay

Yaxchilan: yahsh-chee-lahn

BOOKS TO READ

Ancient America: Cultural Atlas for Young People by Marion Wood (Facts on File, 1990)
This book includes a spread on the city of Palenque and a section on the Maya calendar.

A Mayan Town through History by Xavier Hernàndez (Wayland, 1992)
This gives lots of information on daily life and technology, illustrated with fine line drawings.

The Maya by Robert Nicholson (Two-Can Publishing, 1993)
A colourful children's book about the Maya, including a traditional Maya story.

For Teachers
We Have Always Lived Here by Margaret Burr
An active learning pack, looking at the ancient and modern Maya of Guatemala, published by the Minority Rights Group, London.

INDEX